As the rain hides the s...

Gaelic prayer

IAN ASSERSOHN

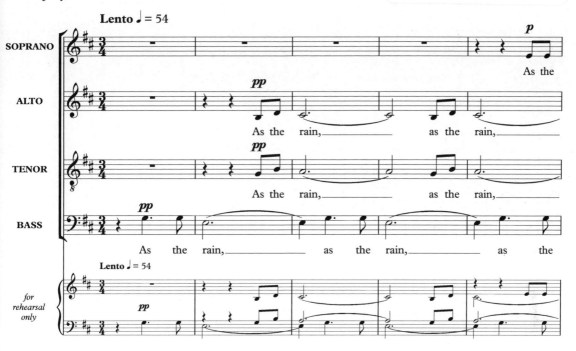

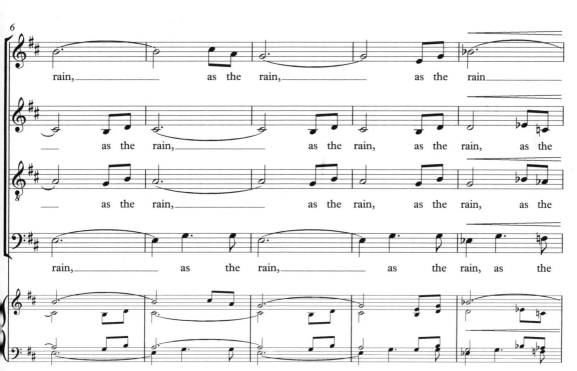

Duration: 5 mins

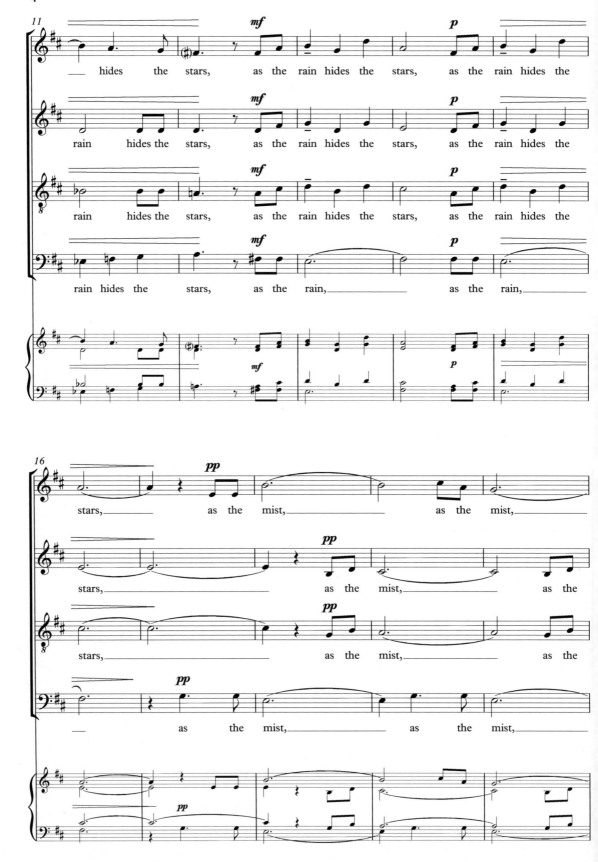

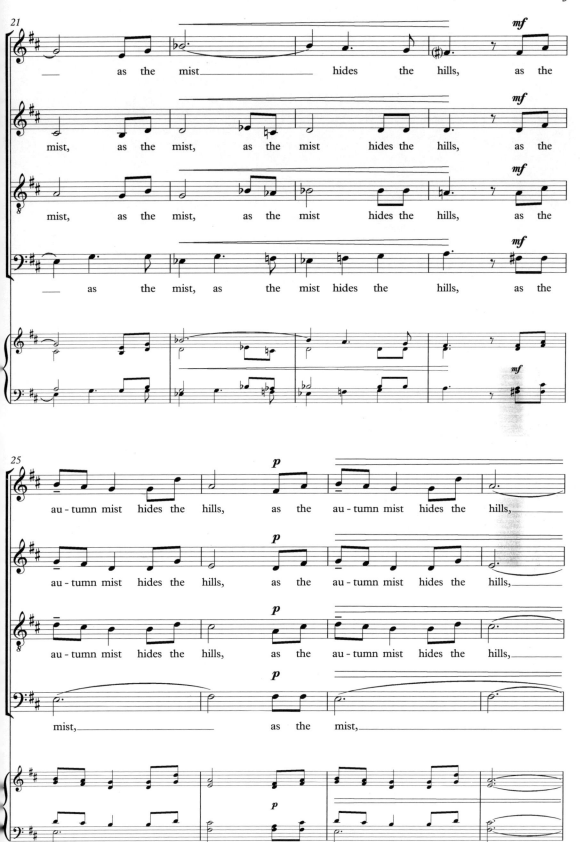

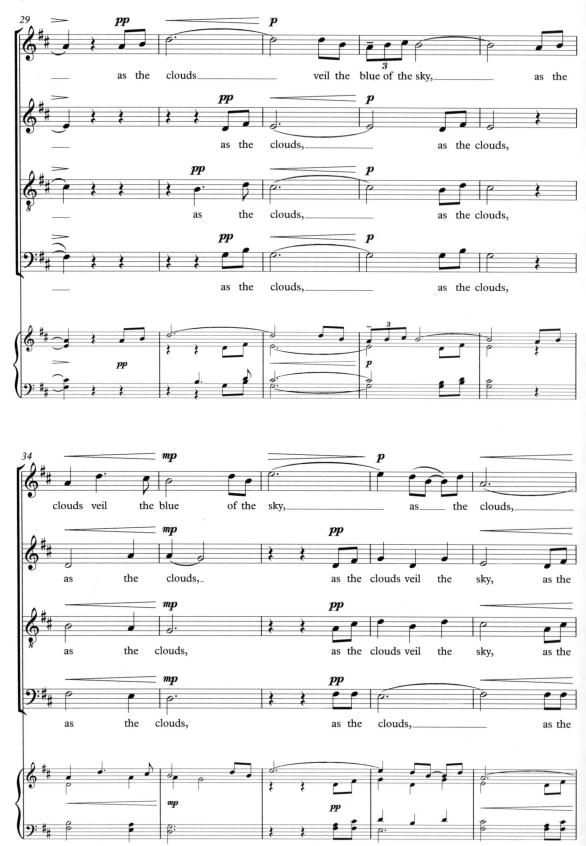

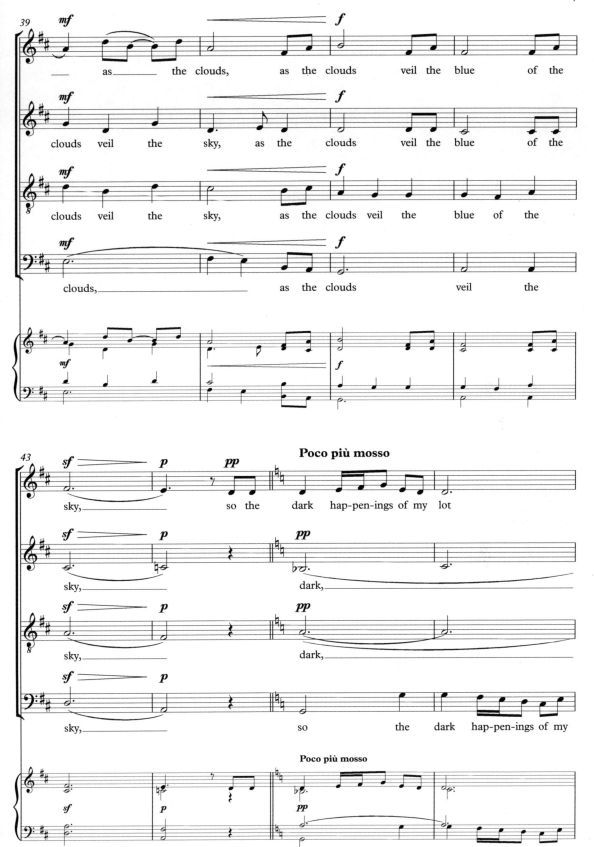

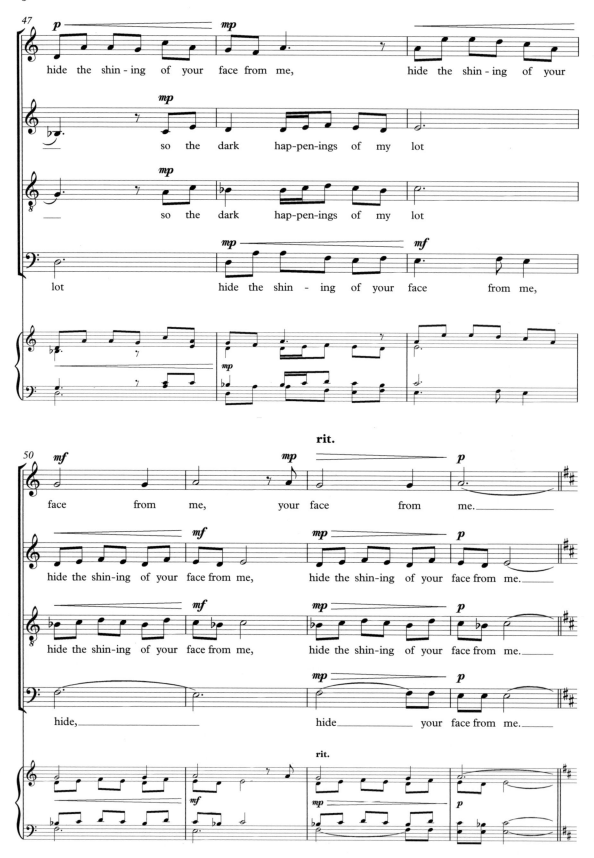

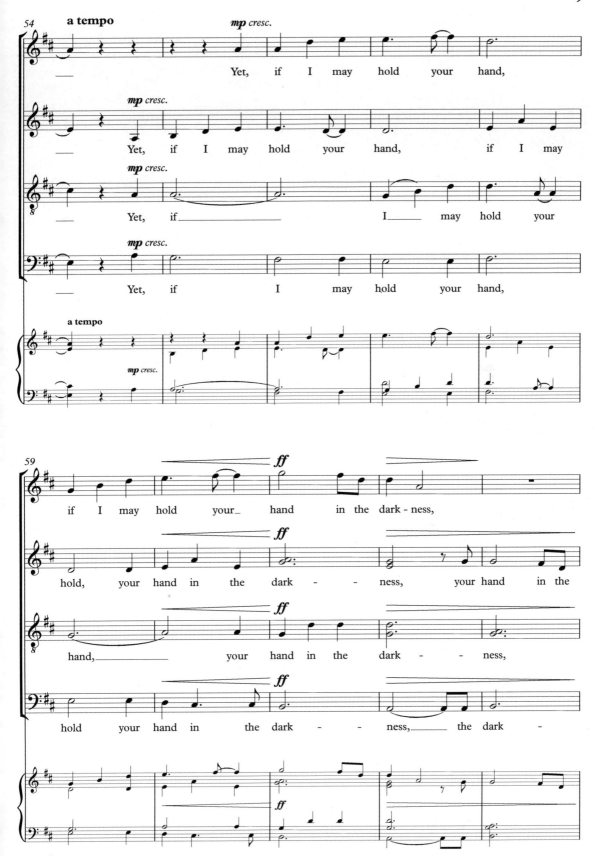

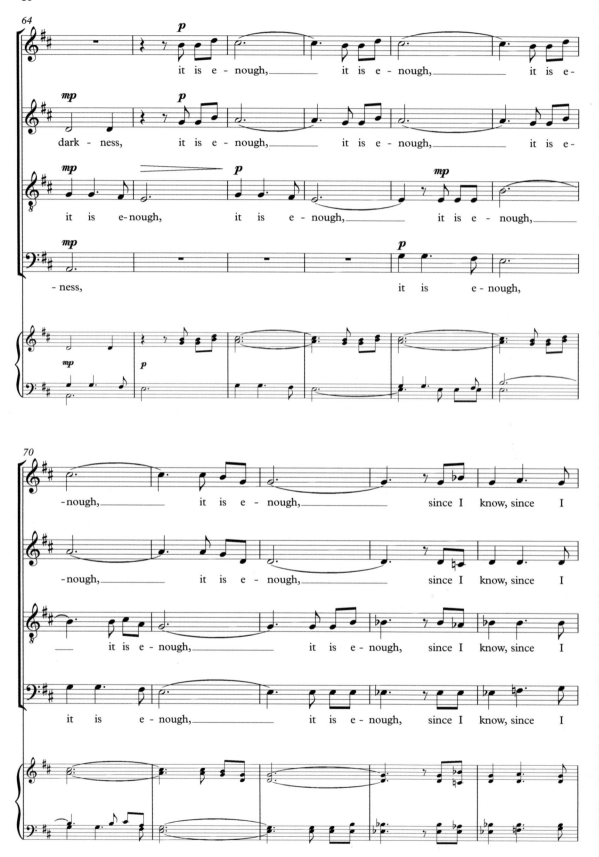

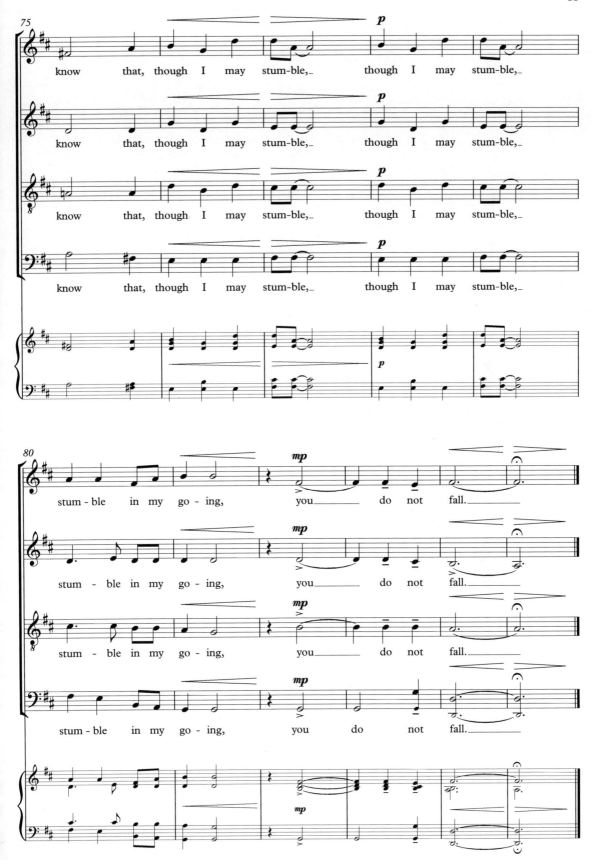

X798 **As the rain hides the stars** ASSERSOHN

OXFORD
UNIVERSITY PRESS

www.oup.com

ISBN 978-0-19-354074-3

9 780193 540743